THE AUTHORITATIVE GUIDE TO EMAIL LIST BUILDING

GROWING REVENUE AND PROFIT THROUGH EMAIL ENGAGEMENT

JESSE TORRES

To my three girls. I can't imagine doing this without you.

CONTENTS

INTRODUCTION

I'll agree that when it comes to digital marketing, email does not have the sex appeal of Facebook, YouTube, Snapchat, Twitter or most other social networks. However, studies prove that email, "the little train that could," continues to chug on down the digital marketing landscape ahead of all others in terms of return on investment (ROI). This book provides seven actionable steps that any business can take to dramatically increase email subscriptions and improve revenue and profits.

During the 2015 Any Lab Test Now! (AnyLabTestNow.com) Annual Franchisee Conference, at which I gave the keynote address along with my business partner Aaron M. Sanchez, I was asked by an attending franchisee, "What one thing can I start doing this afternoon to increase my sales?" Without skipping a beat my response was, "Build your list and work it." Email list building is an often overlooked business practice that costs businesses dearly in new and recurring revenue.

Abrar Mohi Shafee is a young entrepreneur, digital marketing phenom and founder of Blogging Spell (BloggingSpell.com). But youth has not kept Abrar from converting his curiosity for all things digital marketing into a massive knowledgebase fed by research and his own digital marketing efforts. During a guest appearance on the widely read Kissmetrics blog, Abrar summarized the importance of email list building in six words - "Your email is your biggest asset!"

But after all these years and after all the digital innovation we have experienced during the last decade how can email continue to dominate as the 800 pound digital marketing gorilla? The question is more pronounced when you consider the effectiveness of today's email filters. It would seem that with all these changes the effectiveness of email by now would have taken a deep fall off a cliff and that social media marketing would assume the alpha dog role.

According to the experts, a well-designed email marketing program built on a solid list building practice is more valuable than even the sexiest social media marketing campaigns. If done well, a sound email marketing program provides a return on investment unmatched by other digital-marketing efforts.

Digital marketing firm Campaign Monitor wrote in its blog, "Even with the explosion of new technology, marketers keep coming back to email. The reason is clear -- for 10 years in a row, email is the channel generating the highest ROI for marketers. For every $1 spent, email marketing generates $38 in ROI."

Consultancy McKinsey & Company concurs, stating that "Email remains a significantly more effective way to acquire customers than social media - nearly 40 times that of Facebook and Twitter combined. That's because 91 percent of all U.S. consumers still use email daily, and the rate at which emails prompt purchases is not only estimated to be at least three times that of social media, but the average order value is also 17 percent higher."

Bam! Pow! Crack! Take that Mark Zuckerberg.

One of the most prolific bank robbers in United States history was Willie Sutton. He is well known in banking and law enforcement circles for having stolen roughly $2 million in his 40 year criminal career.

If there was one thing Slick Willie had become known for it was his mastery of the obvious. According to legend, during a media interview Willie was asked by a reporter why he robbed banks. "Because that's where the money is!" Brilliant! So obvious and so true.

So why should businesses focus on email list building? Because that's where the money is! It is Sutton's Law and it works.

Shafee states that email "list building is the key to a regal online presence." But a successful email marketing program requires more than just a large email list. A successful email marketing program runs off of a high-quality email list where recipients of emails regularly engage with the business as a result of the emails and do not consider the emails just another piece of spam.

I am shocked by the lack of emphasis placed by small business owners on building a high quality email list given the advantage of email over other digital marketing channels. It is very common in my meetings with small business owners to find that email list building ranks at the bottom of their marketing efforts. This is especially true with brick-and-mortar businesses.

BOLDFACE (BOLDFACEGear.com) is the world's only maker of customized on-demand backpacks. Consumers purchase the backpacks through its website, BOLDFACEGear.com. Success for BOLDFACE is dependent upon the company being able to continually generate a list of interested consumers that are receptive to receiving and acting on marketing emails. For a company such as BOLDFACE, a solid email list building program can literally mean the difference between life and death.

BOLDFACE CEO Randy Fenton stated to me during an interview that some businesses struggle with email list building because "Businesses fear that setting up an email collection strategy that is too aggressive may turn off too many visitors to a website resulting in lost potential customers."

"As an ecommerce business, we rely heavily on email marketing," Fenton added. "Some people will just not provide it, and others will be insulted that we even asked for that information. But they are not likely our target customer or are not likely to make a purchase from us now or in the future. Smart businesses make the ask. No business is going to get every visitor to sign up. But those that do sign up are interested in the products and will hopefully make a purchase at some point."

However, Shafee cautions that "The technique we choose to request emails often affects the user experience. Sometimes it affects it so badly that users decide to leave our site."

While email list building is critical for success, the manner in which emails are requested makes all the difference in building a strong list of prospects. You don't want to build any list. You want to build the right list.

Contained within the following pages are seven techniques that can be implemented immediately on your website to dramatically increase email subscriptions. Now it's time to go build your list and work it!

CREATE AMAZING CONTENT

Kevan Lee wrote in the Buffer Social blog, "Basically, everything begins with content. People will find your site because of your amazing content. They will keep coming back for amazing content. Your amazing content will be the foundation of what you email to them, which will be the reason they stay subscribed (or not.) It all starts with amazing content."

But what is amazing content? The Content Marketing Institute has defined content as something of value and relevant to website visitors intended to "Attract and acquire a clearly defined audience - with the objective of driving profitable customer action."

Amazing content includes great product copy that provides sufficient product details and images to make a visitor comfortable about exactly what the product is, what it looks like and how it works. Amazing content can also be a how-to article that provides step-by-step details about a particular topic. Anything that can convey information (article, whitepaper, video, graphic, etc.) is content. Amazing content takes it to the next level!

Too often website sales copy and articles are too generic and just scratch the surface. In depth and actionable content is of the greatest use. Imagine a YouTube video that thoroughly shows how to use a piece of software or perform a specific action. That is amazing content. Amazing content is any content that gets the website visitor to say, "That content is exactly what I needed. I am definitely better off now."

Let's be honest for a moment – most content on the Internet is awful. It is often poorly conceived, poorly produced, poorly written or more of the same inch-deep, mile-wide "I've-seen-that-already" content. The world does not need more of this content.

A website with poor content has little chance of building a quality email list. Website visitors are smart. They know a valuable site when they see one. If all they get is trash when they visit a website they will move on and never return.

Business owners that attend my digital marketing workshops hear me say repeatedly, "Content is not king. Content is a king maker." In my experience, websites are most successful in generating email subscribers when they create amazing content that addresses the needs of their target audience. Website visitors are looking for content that solves a pain point.

For example, amazing content fills the knowledge gap of a cooking student studying French cuisine. Once the student consumes the content the student is better off. Great content can also show a first-time fisherman how to clean a fish. After consuming the content the visitor has the confidence to prepare the fish without hesitation.

Visitors are attracted to websites based on their lure of solving a pain point. To the extent the content is amazing and addresses the pain point the visitor can more easily be convinced to provide their email address. If the content does not meet the target audience's needs, kiss them goodbye.

"Content gives companies of all sizes the opportunity to engage with somebody," RSL Media's CEO Robert Levin told me during an interview. "It's an opportunity to build a relationship, to build trust and to demonstrate expertise."

But all content is not created equal. Those that take the time to find their target audience's pain points will create an opportunity for engagement. Those that fail to invest the time and energy to create relevant content will sit there wondering why no one is subscribing.

"In today's digital marketplace, producing regular content is critical to any company's success," Joe Issid shared on Monster's website. "The prevalence of social media and the content-driven platforms upon which they rest can reap incalculable benefits for your business."

It's true, all things being equal, more content is better than less content. However, a website will experience superior email subscriptions with less frequent content updates if the content is amazing. Visitors want quality – not garbage. So businesses should focus on quality over quantity – particularly when resources are strained or limited.

As Karen Leland described in *Pinterest for Business: The Basics*, entrepreneurs must effectively "curate content that is meaningful, attractive, social media friendly, and on message with your brand." This involves learning an audience's pain points and creating content that is appealing, sufficiently detailed, and presented in the desired format for consumption.

Christian Jorg, CEO of content-marketing software firm OpenTopic (OpenTopic.com) explained to me during an interview, "The Internet is great because there is so much out there. But it is hard to find the right stuff." It's true. There is definitely a lot of content out there. The problem is that so much of it is garbage.

Since there is so much garbage content out there, it must be working? Otherwise why would websites continue to plaster the Internet with poor quality content? The answer is that websites hosting garbage are not successful. They may exist – but they are not likely effective at growing their subscriber base and creating ongoing engagement that results in revenue and profits. Sooner or later those websites will disappear.

A Nielsen report noted, "Our research suggests that there is a higher degree of trust from consumers when they are reading content from credible, third party experts." In other words, people know and trust websites that provide amazing content. Websites must focus on solving visitors' pain points with amazing content that meets their needs before visitors give away their prized email addresses.

"All companies are now media companies," Levin observed. "Whether you have the ability or desire to spend the money to produce a print magazine, to create a video or simply place content on your website, you no longer need to go to a media company to put out your content." Levin recommended that businesses aiming to create their own content begin with what they know: their audience and their expertise.

Look at other websites that create great content. Identify the factors that make them successful. By studying successful website content you will know what works and what to avoid. Any content development strategy will have hits and misses. Consider visiting or calling professionals (who aren't competitors) to pick their brains about what works.

BE AS CONSPICUOUS AS POSSIBLE

Website visitors demonstrate their interest in a business and its products and services by way of the time they invest browsing website content. The content may be product or service copy, a blog post, a video, a podcast or any other content found on the website. The more time they spend, the more interested they are in an offering or information and the more likely they are to complete a call-to-action such as making a purchase.

But visitors may not be ready or in a position to make an immediate purchase. Some may need to consult a spouse. Others may not have the money but are planning out their purchase once they have it. And others may be just beginning their journey of looking for the right product or service.

A study conducted by Adweek found that 81% of consumers research a product online before making a purchase. So it is common for website visitors to browse, collect information and leave without spending a dime. The world of ecommerce is full of Lookie Lou's.

Business owners should keep in mind that all is not lost in such instances if the business obtains the visitor's email. An email provides business owners with the opportunity to thank the consumer for the visit, offer additional information, make promotional offers and remain top of mind when the consumer is ready to make a purchase.

An effective way to attract new email subscribers is through the placement of conspicuous email subscription opt-in boxes throughout each web page. The opt-in box provides visitors with a convenient method of providing the business with their email address. Once the visitor opts-in the business can begin to create ongoing engagement with subscribers through email campaigns.

A well-designed website provides visitors with ample opt-in opportunities through the placement of opt-in boxes at strategic locations. The greater the number of opt-in reminders, the greater the likelihood that an interested visitor will subscribe. "Big, bold signup forms dominate the home pages of many email-savvy blogs," writes Kevan Lee.

But successfully obtaining email addresses involves more than just throwing up opt-in boxes. To me there is nothing more annoying than visiting a website and being continuously interrupted by pop-up boxes asking for an email address. Fortunately there are techniques that businesses can use to keep email subscription top-of-mind with visitors without being overly disruptive.

The trick to growing an email list is to provide useful information that engages visitors and gets visitors to want more. In the 1989 movie, *Field of Dreams*, Ray Kinsella hears a voice coming from the corn field saying, "If you build it, he will come." While merely building a baseball diamond was enough to attract Shoeless Joe Jackson to the baseball field, simply adding opt-in boxes to a website will not be enough to drive subscriptions. Before consumers give up their valuable email address they want to make sure that they will receive something of value in exchange. They want amazing content! If the website is of zero value to them they will move on and not provide any information.

"In analyzing the websites and techniques of some of these awesome email list builders, a certain formula started to emerge," writes Kevan Lee on the Buffer Social blog. "If I could boil down the process of building a massive email list to just the most basic parts, I think it would look like this: Amazing Blog Content + Crystal Clear Calls-to-Action = Massive Email List."

"It's an inescapable truth that everyone you want to reach has 1,440 minutes in their day; not a minute more," writes Stef Gonzaga in the Boost Blog Traffic blog. "Unless they see the value of joining your list, they simply won't invest any of those valuable minutes in you and your blog."

Assuming the website provides amazing content, business owners should feel confident with the placement of subscriber opt-in boxes at three key locations to encourage email subscriptions: the top of the page, the sidebar and the bottom of the page.

Placement at these locations is non-disruptive and ensures that the visitor is continuously reminded to opt-in throughout the visit. Using this approach eliminates the visitor's need to figure out how to subscribe, and it does not interrupt the visitor as the boxes are built into the design of the web page.

Email management companies such as MailChimp (MailChimp.com), Aweber (Aweber.com) and Constant Contact (ConstantContact.com) make the process of creating opt-in boxes extremely painless for business owners. These companies provide plug-ins that are compatible with most websites, including websites built using the popular Wordpress (WordPress.org) and Shopify (Shopify.com) content management systems. The process can take less than an hour to set up.

The three recommended locations for the opt-in boxes are standard. In recent times, other techniques used to display opt-in boxes have surfaced. The effectiveness of these emerging techniques can vary from website to website, based upon the effect they have on visitors. As such, there is no single method to display opt-in boxes.

For example, some websites use static opt-in box plugins such as Conversion Insights' (ConversionInsights.net) Attention Grabber while others use floating opt-in boxes such as Hello Bar (HelloBar.com). Companies such as OptinMonster (OptinMonster.com) take opt-in boxes to the next level with options such as slide-ins, time-delayed pop-ups and even opt-in boxes that appear when the visitor shows signs of leaving the page (exit intent).

As long as email continues to dominate the field of digital marketing, firms will continue to innovate the email opt-in process.

The Golden Rule of opt-in boxes is to offer the opt-in as often as possible without overwhelming, annoying or distracting the visitor. According to Kevan Lee, "Fortunately, there are options for popups, as the strategy covers a wide variety of different implementations." Lee describes the following as the eight preferred static and dynamic opt-in box locations:

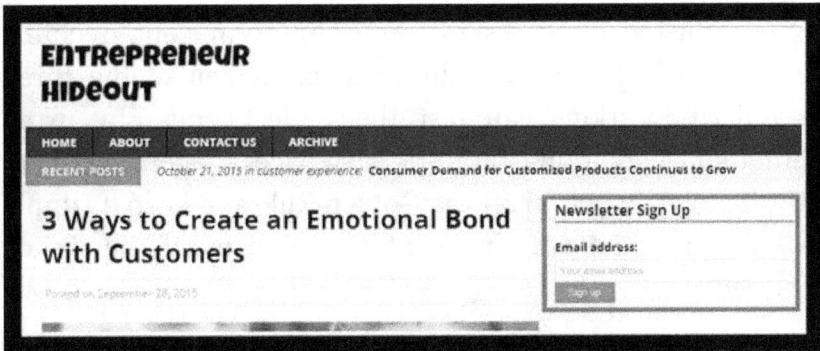

EXAMPLE OF SIDEBAR OPT-IN BOX

1. Top Menu Bar

2. Header of Website

3. In the Byline

4. Sidebar

5. Inside the Blog Content

6. Footer of the Content

7. Popup/Popover

8. Author Bio

Entrepreneurs should leverage social media to develop their companies' voice. A thoughtful social-media strategy can turn a company into more of a friend and less of a business.

If you enjoyed this article subscribe to our mailing list

Email Address

Subscribe

EXAMPLE OF OPT-IN BOX AT FOOTER OF CONTENT

Business owners interested in trying out dynamic email opt-in boxes in addition to or in lieu of the three standard locations can test their effectiveness by using different techniques on different pages, when possible. Ultimately, do not forget the Golden Rule and keep it simple - and make the amazing content the focus of the visitor interaction.

LIMIT THE INFORMATION COLLECTED

In a perfect world, business owners would collect every bit of data possible from website visitors, including email, name, physical address, cell phone number and on and on. But the reality is that consumers are just not comfortable giving up a lot of information about themselves.

"After all, if it gets into the wrong hands, they could be opening the door to spam emails, phishing attempts, and other vulgar assaults on their inbox," writes Gonzaga.

Andy Crestodina writes in the Orbit Media Studios blog that websites must "Assure the subscriber that they won't receive spam and that you won't share their information with anyone else." Also, if products or services are sold on the website there should be other assurances such as security certifications from firms such as TRUSTe and its Web Privacy Program (Truste.com). Also helpful is ratings from firms such as the Better Business Bureau (BBB.org).

Consumers also fear that their information will be involved in a hacking incident. The greater the amount of information captured during an opt-in, the greater the risk to visitors. The possibility of having their information stolen and used in identity theft schemes discourages website visitors from volunteering too much information.

And the risk is real. In 2014 alone, hackers stole information from some of the country's largest organizations, including Home Depot, Target, Best Buy, eBay, PF Chang's, Subway, JP Morgan Chase and Bank of America.

As a result, it is not difficult to scare away potential subscribers. Asking for too much information too soon drives them away, leaving the business with nothing to show for the engagement. And it also hurts the visitor, who loses out on the opportunity to receive valuable information about a product/service of interest.

An opt-in box that limits the information solely to email address will be the most palatable to cautious visitors. While it is always more beneficial to collect at least the subscriber's first name in order to personalize email campaigns, it is often better to collect only the email address and avoid the risk of scaring off the visitor. Businesses can attempt to collect additional information later in the relationship as the subscriber gains confidence in the business and establishes a relationship through regular engagement.

SELL IT WITH SOCIAL PROOF

There is nothing like social proof to boost email opt-in subscriptions. Bar owners create social proof by keeping people in line. "If the line is that long, that must be the cool place to hang out," say passers-by as they get into line.

According to the ZenSpill blog, "We are social creatures by nature. No one wants to feel like they are the only subscriber of your blog. Having some social proof in your optin form or near it will give your readers the feeling that they are making the right choice by subscribing."

My eleven year-old daughter is a good example of social proof at work. Last winter I thought it would be great if she participated in the Los Angeles County Junior Lifeguard Program. We live near the ocean and she spends a lot of time at the beach. She also loves swimming and surfing. Since the Junior Lifeguard Program takes place on the beach for an entire month in the summer I thought it was a perfect summer activity.

When I brought up the idea my daughter poo-poo'd it. She thought it was too much physical work for the summer break – a time that she thought would be dedicated to sitting on a beach chair, watching the waves and gossiping with her friends.

One day in the spring my daughter came home from school and informed my wife and I that she was going to begin training for the Junior Lifeguards tryout. When I asked why she suddenly wanted to join the Junior Lifeguards she said that all her friends were going to do it…and more importantly, that you got to wear the blue Junior Lifeguards sweatshirt that the older kids wear around town.

My daughter zero. Social proof one. There's nothing more powerful than social proof when attempting to persuade someone to do something – including an email opt-in.

Ed Hallen, co-founder of Klavivo (Klavivo.com), an ecommerce email marketing firm defined social proof on a Buffer Social blog post as, "The concept that people will conform to the actions of others under the assumption that those actions are reflective of the correct behavior."

ZenSpill identifies the following as three effective approaches to using social proof on a website:

- **Authority Figures:** Making reference to people, companies or other entities that people trust gives the website bono fides that encourage visitors to subscribe. For example, if a business works with a major influencer or a respected and recognized company (e.g., Apple and Google), including a testimonial or making reference to this fact may encourage subscribers. Adding the logo of a recognized brand works wonders when it comes to social proof. "If Apple and Google think they are good, they must be good enough for little old me." Clear any testimonial or reference with the source before posting it on the website. Some people and organizations may have policies against such endorsements.

- **Subscriber Count:** Websites with large subscriber lists should boast about it. People hate being left out. A website that has over 10,000 subscribers can easily make it to 11,000 subscribers by posting something along the lines of "Join over 10,000 subscribers." This approach works well for websites that have a large subscriber base. Those with small subscriber numbers should not use this approach as there is nothing impressive about 10, 50 or 100 subscribers. And it may work against a website as visitors may opine that there is a reason that so few people subscribe. So businesses should build their list before using subscriber count as a form of social proof.

- **Social Media:** Similar to subscriber count, using social media followers is a great way to boast about a website's popularity. Plug-ins such as Social Count Plus (WordPress.org/plugins/social-count-plus) show visitors how many followers a website has on the various social media platforms.

"The opinions of 'other' people are more believable and persuasive than what you've got to say about yourself," writes Amanda Leclair in the Impact Branding & Design blog. "Use that to your advantage. Display social proof proudly on your site."

Amanda notes additional social proof techniques that help with email subscriptions, including product reviews and star ratings from users, awards, customer photos and videos, customer success stories, case studies and trust badges.

Businesses must ensure that their websites are optimized to encourage opt-in email subscriptions through the use of social proof. With social proof, subscribers beget subscribers. The idea is to get visitors to say, "If they loved the content, I'll love it too! Let's do this!"

USE FREEBIES

Who doesn't love free stuff? Free fries with the burger. Free dessert with your meal. Kids eat free. It doesn't matter what it is, we love free!

Freebies don't just work with food. Freebies also work well when building an email list. Visitors to a website may not be willing to give up their email address until they realize they can get something valuable in exchange for their email currency. If the offer is right the email address is yours!

"To break through your reader's defenses, you must offer something genuinely tempting. Something of real value," states Stef Gonzaga. "Something they would even pay for – if you weren't so generously giving it away in exchange for their email address."

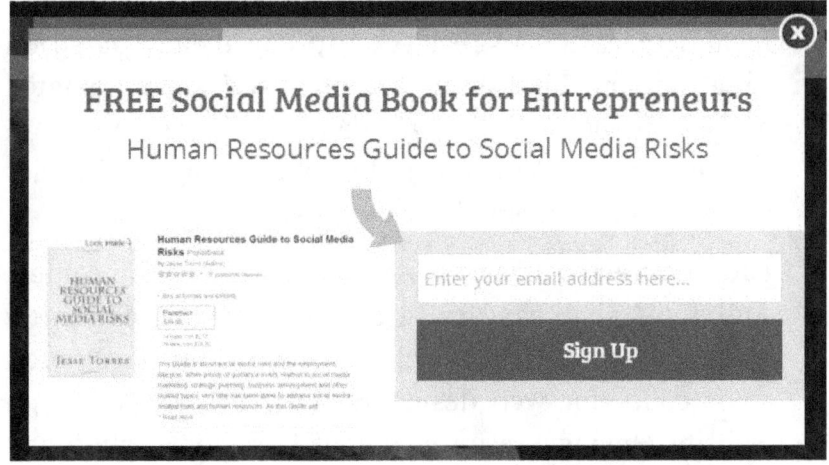

EXAMPLE OF CALL TO ACTION USING FREEBIE

A common approach used to encourage opt-in subscriptions is offering an ebook, white paper, video or other content that is of value to visitors. The best way to determine the content to offer is to understand the website's target audience and what that audience considers valuable. For example, visitors to Entrepreneur Hideout (EntrepreneurHideout.com) are offered an ebook geared to small business owners.

Gonzaga offers the following nine ideas for freebies that visitors will exchange for their email address. These are her ideas. Each website audience is different and as such, other types of freebies may be more effective. Businesses should test different freebies to determine what works best.

- **Email Series:** One of the great innovations of email companies such as MailChimp and Aweber is their ability to deliver a series of preset emails to specific email lists on a predetermined schedule (e.g., every day, every week, etc.). With this functionality it is possible to create an email series the meets the needs of visitors. For example, visitors to an app coding website can opt-in and in exchange receive a 10-day email course on Creating Your First App. The email series is automated and set to begin delivering daily emails as soon as a visitor opts-in. With the right content an email series will attract lots of email subscribers.

- **Cheat Sheets:** Time saving tools are always welcomed. Any tools that can fast track success are extremely valuable. An example of a cheat sheet is a list of common color codes for web designers that visit a web design website. Having a resource that can provide a solution at a glance saves time and is worthy of an email subscription.

- **Templates:** Templates are always popular freebies. Why reinvent the wheel when visitors can get a template that saves time. Saving time is the same as saving money. A job search website can do well by providing a set of resume templates that can be used for different scenarios. Using a template that is of interest to visitors can dramatically increase email subscriptions.

- **Blueprints/Roadmaps:** The shortest distance between two points is a straight line. Unfortunately, too often we waste valuable time figuring out how to navigate a challenge. Offering visitors the opportunity to save valuable time by providing a tested roadmap is a great way to encourage email subscriptions.

- **Case Studies:** There is no question that failure is a valuable tool. But why fail for failure's sake? Providing visitors with case studies the feature what worked and what did not is a great resource to anyone seeking success. For example, a case study that addresses how a company achieved 500% sales growth through email marketing would be an extremely valuable tool for any business. Many visitors will consider the cost of an email a small price to pay for the amazing intelligence contained in the case study.

- **Video Courses:** According to Justin Ferriman in the Learn Dash blog, there are seven ways people learn: visual; physical; aural; verbal; logical; social; and, solitary. Those that prefer to learn visually can be provided with a video course. For example, an auto repair website can provide a video course on how to connect a laptop to a car's onboard computer to measure a car's vitals. A video course is great not only for those that prefer visual learning but it also is a great way to demonstrate proper use of the diagnostic software used to take the car's readings. Along with video courses and the email series noted above, another option that can be offered to visitors is a podcast course - for those that prefer verbal learning. Making the information available in a preferred-learning format will go a long way in driving up email subscriptions.

- **Manifestos:** "A manifesto is a written public declaration of your principles and beliefs. It's inspirational in nature and a persuasive way to establish the tone and point of view of your blog from the beginning," writes Gonzaga. Websites that have a serious mission and vision and are committed to carrying it out can make use of the manifesto. For example, a website dedicated to ensuring that no citizen is denied the opportunity to learn computer programming skills can issue a manifesto to visitors that are in sync with the website's mission and vision. The manifesto, while not right for every website, is a great way to build a strong and engaged email subscriber base.

- **Graphical Giveaways:** Depending on the website's target audience, graphics are sometimes attractive freebies. For example, a website that caters to graphic designers may offer icons or other images that can be freely used by email subscribers.

- **Toolkits:** A toolkit is the ultimate freebie. Imagine creating a resource that contained a cheat sheet, a template, a blueprint, a case study and a video and audio course and offering it all as a single freebie. That would make for an irresistible bribe worthy of anyone's email address.

Providing freebies creates a win/win solution to the opt-in challenge by giving visitors something they value in exchange for something the business values. The exchange may also create goodwill in the mind of the visitor, making the visitor more receptive to engaging with future emails.

CONTENT UPGRADES

Visit most popular ecommerce sites and chances are that within five seconds you will be prompted for your email address in exchange for a freebie. Typical freebies include coupons, checklists, ebooks, infographics or some other content. There's nothing wrong with offering such freebies in exchange for an email as it provides mutual benefit. Anything that improves email subscriptions and benefits both parties is a good thing. Particularly when taking into consideration that many of today's businesses live and die by the sales generated from their email marketing efforts. Unfortunately, despite their no-cost feature, freebies often fail to generate high email subscription rates.

In theory, freebies are a great tool to attract email subscriptions. They appeal to consumers' deep rooted need for useful free stuff. But for many, freebies are often too generic and just not useful enough to exchange for a valuable email address. Today's discriminating website visitors are on a mission to find very specific information. Anything short of meeting their needs results in them bouncing from your website and onto the next. But don't worry. There is a strategy that can be put into place to capture these visitors. This strategy looks a lot like the freebie strategy. It's called the "content upgrade" strategy and it works likes nothing else.

Consider this example: an online vitamin and supplement business offers visitors in exchange for their email, a freebie comprised of Top 10 Ultra Fat Burning

Exercises. The offer to receive this Top 10 List is displayed via pop up box and the offer is made to all website visitors regardless of the web page they visit. The business assumes that fat loss and exercise are two subjects of interest to most visitors and as such, many visitors will find the generic offer useful and prompt a subscription.

Now imagine that a visitor to the website, using a search engine, lands on a page about abdominal exercises. The visitor, an amateur body builder, is looking for tips on developing more defined abdominals through exercise – not losing body fat. As a result, the offer of 10 fat burning exercises is of no interest and the visitor does not subscribe, causing the business to lose out on capturing a valuable asset – the email address.

But what if following the article on abdominal exercises there was an offer specifically tailored to the information contained in the abdominal exercise article. Imagine if the offer was access to a video that demonstrated the proper technique associated with the exercises contained in the article. Would the business have a greater likelihood of capturing a visitor's email address in this case? Most definitely!

In this example the offer moves beyond a generic freebie to a content-specific freebie referred to as a "content upgrade." The content upgrade provides information that expands upon the original content (the abdominal article), making it much more targeted and relevant and much more worthy of exchanging for an email address.

The content upgrade can take any form – text, video, audio or a combination. It can be something as basic as a checklist or as complex as a set of training videos. What is most important is that the content upgrade relates specifically to the original content and improves upon that content.

In the example above the visitor was interested in abdominal exercises. The generic Top 10 list was not sufficiently persuasive to convince the visitor to subscribe. However, when presented with a video (the content upgrade) based on the content contained in the article, the visitor is more likely to subscribe as the offer relates specifically to the visitor's interests.

"People have done this and they have gotten insane amounts of conversions. Almost 400% to 500% more," said Arvindh Sunder on the digipodcast podcast. David Risley, host of the Coffee Break Blogging podcast and founder of BlogMarketingAcademy.com, stated on his podcast that a content upgrade is "The absolute most effective opt-in strategy for a blog." Risley continued by stating that "It needs to be highly specific. It needs to be very tightly related to that blog post."

"A content upgrade should be a natural outflow of that post...It has to be baked into it. It can't just be an appendage you add at the end," said Bryan Harris of VideoFruit.com during an interview on The Authority Hacker podcast. "It has to be part of the whole soul of the post. When you do that you'll see substantial upticks."

Of course, the obvious question is "Doesn't this strategy require more work on my part?" The answer is, yes! A content upgrade involves the creation of a new piece of content. However, while the effort in creating the content may be similar to the effort in creating the content upon which the content upgrade is based, the return on investment of a content upgrade is many times better than ordinary content. The subscription rate on a content upgrade will produce email subscriptions many times greater than other opt-in strategies. Also, to the extent that it makes sense, the same content upgrade can be used with other website content.

John Jantsch provided the following seven ideas for content upgrades in his Duct Tape Marketing Blog. These are his favorites. Visitor preferences can vary from website to website so different forms of content should be tested to determine what resonates best with visitors.

- **Checklists**: To the extent that content can be summarized into a checklist, this tool can literally improve the life of the visitor. Checklists should compartmentalize the original content and convert it into a list that helps guide the user through a process. The more complex the process, the more helpful the checklist. There is nothing like a checklist to give someone the confidence that a job was performed thoroughly and that nothing fell through the cracks.

- **Templates**: Templates are incredibly helpful tools. A template, when applicable, does wonders in getting an activity off the ground. For example, a template that lays out the proper form of a pitch email to journalists makes to perfect complement to an article related to contacting journalists. The more battle-tested the template, the more valuable it is to visitors and the more likely it will result in large-scale opt-in subscriptions.

- **List of Tools**: Whether it is eating right, losing weight or gaining publicity, the right tool can be the difference between success and failure. If visitors are serious about taking action then they will be very eager to give up their email address in exchange for a curated list of tools that helps them with the execution.

- **List of Links**: Just as the list of tools inspires visitors to subscribe, so does a great list of links. Imagine a product page selling vitamin C. Now imagine that the product page contained an offer to links providing articles about foods that maximize absorption of vitamin C. Someone interested in vitamin C would definitely be interested in learning how to maximize its absorption.

- **Video or Screen Shots**: The number one question I get after my email subscription workshop is something along the lines of, "Can you show me exactly how to place an opt-in box on my blog. I have never done this before and it seems complicated." This is where my word document containing step-by-step screen shots is helpful. Offering a visual tool is a great way to bribe visitors for their email.

- **Swipe File or Toolbox:** A content upgrade containing scripts, email templates, forms or other tools related to an article is priceless. Imagine an article written for gadget repair businesses about replacing the glass cover of mobile phones. Now imagine a content upgrade that provides step-by-step details for every major phone on the market. That is definitely something worth exchanging for an email!

- **Top 10 List:** When all else fails, there is always the Top 10 List. A solid list of great resources tightly associated with the content is always a winner when it comes to gaining email subscribers.

In an ideal world a website would provide a content upgrade to accompany every item of content. Unfortunately, this strategy is not always feasible – particularly for small businesses short on resources. The following are three tips to guide a small business through a content upgrade strategy.

1. Focus on popular content.

Brian Dean, founder of Backlinko, advises on his blog that businesses identify the highest traffic pages as candidates for content upgrades. Once the pages are identified the business should determine the best type of content upgrade to offer. This strategy ensures that resources are dedicated to web pages that provide the greatest bang for the buck.

2. Use graphics to drive conversions.

In an effort to improve conversion Risley recommends the use of images as part of the content upgrade's call-to-action. For example, a red button at the bottom of a web page stating "Download My Report" attracts attention and will encourage a higher click-through rate than simple text. Other examples can include images of books for ebook upgrades, a video still image for videos or other similar graphics.

3. Use tools to deliver the content upgrades.

When rolling out a content upgrade strategy it is recommended that businesses use a service such as Lead Pages (LeadPages.net) to manage the delivery of content upgrades. These services allow businesses to quickly design and roll out web pages called "lead pages" that are used to describe the offer, collect the email and deliver the promised content. These services provide a seamless experience for both the business and the subscriber.

HOST A CONTEST

If everything else fails (don't worry, it won't!) host the "sure thing" – a contest! According to Emily Dowdle in the OptinMonster blog, "Everyone loves to win something. You'd be surprised how much people are willing to do just to win a t-shirt."

BOLDFACE's Fenton adds, "Every few months we'll hold a giveaway for a backpack or guitar bag. We use a lead page to collect the email. At the end of the contest our cost per lead is pennies. Our winner gets an amazing BOLDFACE product and we retarget all participants with post-contest offers to incent a purchase. It's an amazing way to lift email subscriptions and sales."

Todd Giannattasio breaks it down nicely on the Tresnic Media blog, "The offer that you make for your audience has to be of value to them, but also related to the products or services that your business offers. If you are running an auto parts store and want to grow your fan base, offering a free iPad would be great incentive to sign up for your contest, but that doesn't mean those people are going to be quality customers. They will more than likely sign up for your sweepstakes and then unsubscribe after the contest is over."

In the case of BOLDFACE, the backpack and guitar bag company offers one of their products. Using their products as the bribe provides an email list of individuals interested specifically in BOLDFACE products. The direct tie-in provides a list of emails belonging to individuals actually interested in the products and services. This makes later marketing much more effective.

"To collect the most email addresses, promote the contest across all your platforms: your website, social media pages and emails," writes Dowdle.

<u>CLOSING</u>

I have experienced phenomenal results using these seven techniques. It is no exaggeration when I state that one website I operate saw an immediate 10X increase in email subscriptions.

Implementing these techniques is not an overnight activity. My recommendation is to sit down and evaluate how each of the strategies can be implemented on your website. Prioritize according to resources and do not stop until all seven strategies are in place.

I hope you have found this book helpful. I tried to keep it short and focused. If you have comments or suggestions I ask that you email me directly at Jesse@JesseTorres.com.

In the spirit of email subscriptions I invite you to register for my Email Subscription Tips, Tricks and Hacks Newsletter. Visit www.JesseTorres.com/TTH to sign up.

ABOUT THE AUTHOR

Jesse Torres has spent over 20 years in leadership and executive management positions at small and large firms. Jesse has written many books and articles related to entrepreneurship, marketing and social media. Jesse is a contributing writer for Entrepreneur, Top 100 Business Blogger according to BizHumm, frequent speaker and is often interviewed by business publications. Jesse has testified before the United States House of Representatives on behalf of America's small businesses and is a graduate of UCLA. Jesse lives with his wife and two daughters in Manhattan Beach, California.

Jesse has authored several books, including the Human Resources Guide to Social Media Risks, Community Bankers Guide to Social Network Marketing, Community Bankers Guide to Hispanic Marketing and Creating an Ironclad Social Media Policy.

Jesse can be reached by email at Jesse@JesseTorres.com.

BIBLIOGRAPHY

Aufreiter, Nora, Julien Boudet, and Vivian Weng, "Why marketers
should keep sending you e-mails," *McKinsey & Company*,
January 2014, *http:/mckinsey.com/business-
functions/marketing-and-sales/our-insights/why-marketers-
should-keep-sending-you-emails.*

Crestodina, Andy, "Email Signup Forms: 4 Things That Lead to
Huge Success or Total Failure," *Orbit Media Studios Blog*,
https://www.orbitmedia.com/blog/email-signup-forms/.

Dean, Brian, "How To Boost Conversions by 785% in One Day
(The Content Upgrade)," *Backlinko*, November 25, 2015,
http://backlinko.com/increase-conversions.

Dowdle, Emily, "How to Double Your Email Subscribers Right
Now," *OptinMonster Blog*, October 2, 2014,

http://optinmonster.com/how-to-double-your-email-subscribers-right-now/.

Ferriman, Justin, "7 Major Learning Styles – Which One are You?," *LearnDash*, May 17, 2013, *http://www.learndash.com/7-major-learning-styles-which-one-is-you/*.

Gonzaga, Stef. "9 Irresistible Incentives That'll Grow Your Email List Like Crazy," *Boost Blog Traffic Blog,* April 10, 2014, *http://boostblogtraffic.com/email-list-incentives/*.

Hallen, Ed, "The Science of Social Proof: 5 Types and the Psychology Behind Why They Work," *BufferSocial Blog*, May 1, 2014, *https://blog.bufferapp.com/the-ultimate-guide-to-social-proof*.

Issid, Joe, "Why Your Business Should Curate Content," *Monster Blog*, *http://hiring.monster.ca/hr/hr-best-practices/recruiting-hiring-advice/strategic-workforce-planning/content-curation-ca.aspx*.

Jantsch, John, "Content Upgrades Are The New Gold Standard For Lead Capture," *Duct Tape Marketing*, http://www.ducttapemarketing.com/blog/content-upgrade/.

Leclair, Amanda, "3 Things to Keep in Mind When Using Social Proof On Your Landing Pages," *Impact Branding & Design Blog*, August 5, 2015, *https://www.impactbnd.com/blog/3-tips-for-boosting-landing-page-conversions-by-leveraging-social-proof*.

Lee, Kevan, "Email List-Building From the Experts: How to Grow a Massive Email List," *BufferSocial Blog*, June 5, 2014, *https://blog.bufferapp.com/email-list-building*.

Leland, Karen, "Pinterest for Business: The Basics: eBook Short: Task-Specific Solutions for Business Entrepreneurs," Amazon Digital Services, LLC, April 23, 2013.

Morrison, Kimberlee, "81% of Shoppers Conduct Online Research Before Buying," Social Times, November 28, 2014, http://www.adweek.com/socialtimes/81-shoppers-conduct-online-research-making-purchase-infographic/208527.

Shafee, Abrar Mohi, "10 Ways to Capture Email Leads Without Disturbing Your Visitors," *Kissmetrics Blog*, *https://blog.kissmetrics.com/capture-email-leads/*.

"Bryan Harris on Building An Email List, Content Upgrades and Selling to Your List," *Authority Hacker Podcast*, *https://soundcloud.com/authorityhacker/rebroadcast-bryan-harris-on*.

"Content Upgrades And How To Use Them For List Building," *Blog Marketing Academy*, *http://www.blogmarketingacademy.com/content-upgrades-and-how-to-use-them-for-list-building/*.

"Getting Started With Content Upgrades," *digipodcast*, January 6, 2016, *http://digipodcast.com/content-upgrades/*.

"How To Grow Your Email List by 254% In 3 Months With A Facebook Contest,"*Tresnic Media*, https://tresnicmedia.com/how-to-grow-your-email-list-by-254-in-3-months-with-a-facebook-contest-case-study/.

"How To Grow Your Email Subscription By 400%," *ZenSpill*, http://www.zenspill.com/how-to-increase-your-email-subscription/.

"Money Talk Interview with Christian Jorg - CEO of OpenTopic," *Money Talk with Jesse Torres*, November 23, 2014, *https://www.youtube.com/watch?v=PIHnZkw1jUM/*.

"Money Talk Interview with Robert Levin - CEO of RSL Media," *Money Talk with Jesse Torres*, November 26, 2014, *https://www.youtube.com/watch?v=Drc2QRN6R_o*.

"The New Rules of Email Marketing," *Campaign Monitor Blog*, *http:/campaignmonitor.com/resources/guides/email-marketing-new-rules/*.

"The Role of Content in the Consumer Decision Making Process," *Nielsen*, March 2014, *http://cdn2.hubspot.net/hub/391049/file-987508079-pdf/Nielsen_inPowered_FINAL.pdf*.

"What is Content Marketing?," *Content Marketing Institute Blog*, *http://contentmarketinginstitute.com/what-is-content-marketing/*.

www.ingramcontent.com/pod-product-compliance
Lightning Source LLC
Chambersburg PA
CBHW070417190526
45169CB00003B/1290